THE YEAR OF SHARING

What will the world be like five hundred years from now? Will cities become bigger and bigger, with more buildings, more cars, more factories, more noise and smoke and dirt? Will there be any green forests left, where animals can live and die in freedom?

Richard's future world is very different from this. There are no cars, only bicycles. There are no cities, only villages. And the forests of the world are only for the wild animals that have always lived there.

Everyone in the world must do their Year of Sharing when they are twelve years old, and by tomorrow morning Richard will be somewhere deep in the forest. He will have a new family – a family of wild animals, and he will live with them for one year. He will be cold and hungry and tired, but he will learn – learn to share the world with other animals.

It is a hard lesson to learn, and there are many dangers waiting in the forest . . .

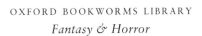

OXFORD BOOKWORMS LIBRARY
Fantasy & Horror

The Year of Sharing

Stage 2 (700 headwords)

Series Editor: Jennifer Bassett
Founder Editor: Tricia Hedge
Activities Editors: Jennifer Bassett and Alison Baxter

For Eva

HARRY GILBERT

The Year of Sharing

OXFORD UNIVERSITY PRESS

OXFORD

UNIVERSITY PRESS

Great Clarendon Street, Oxford OX2 6DP

Oxford University Press is a department of the University of Oxford.
It furthers the University's objective of excellence in research, scholarship,
and education by publishing worldwide in

Oxford New York

Auckland Cape Town Dar es Salaam Hong Kong Karachi
Kuala Lumpur Madrid Melbourne Mexico City Nairobi
New Delhi Shanghai Taipei Toronto

With offices in

Argentina Austria Brazil Chile Czech Republic France Greece
Guatemala Hungary Italy Japan Poland Portugal Singapore
South Korea Switzerland Thailand Turkey Ukraine Vietnam

OXFORD and OXFORD ENGLISH are registered trade marks of
Oxford University Press in the UK and in certain other countries

ISBN 978 0 19 479077 2

A complete recording of this Bookworms edition of
The Year of Sharing is available on audio CD ISBN 978 0 19 479000 0

Typeset by Wyvern Typesetting Ltd, Bristol

Printed in China

Illustrated by: Gerry Grace

Word count (main text): 6390 words

For more information on the Oxford Bookworms Library,
visit www.oup.com/bookworms

CONTENTS

1. A goodbye party

Is somebody listening to this? If there is, hello.

There's a party going on. There are four of us doing our Year of Sharing this year – four of us who are twelve years old. The party is for all their family and friends.

I keep touching my nose. That's where they put the recorder. I can't feel it in my nose, but it's there. It will record all my words when I speak, and any other sounds which are near me. The recorder will go on working for one year.

Can you hear the sounds of the party? Music, talking, laughing, dancing. Is everybody happy?

The answer is no. Everybody has their Year of Sharing when they're twelve, and half of them don't come back. They die. This is a goodbye party.

Perhaps you think I'm afraid. Well, I'm not. I'm the only person here who has no friends or family at the party. I didn't ask any friends to come. My mother's too busy (as usual). I specially asked my father *not* to come – he would cry. I don't want people to see him crying.

I'm going outside. I don't want to talk to anybody.

I can't count all the bicycles by the wall here – half the village is at this party! I didn't bring my bicycle because I'm not going home after the party.

Half the village is at this party!

I would really like a car, not a bicycle, because I love to go fast. I've seen cars in old films, but there are no cars in the world now – no cars, no roads, no factories, no big towns, just little villages like this one. In the old days, they say, the world was a bad and dirty place and animals were dying because of all those cars and factories. Was that really true? I don't know.

Now the world is very boring. We live quietly in our villages, we don't eat meat, and we make everything ourselves with our hands.

I'm sitting outside alone. I've always been alone and that's OK. I'm clever, fast and strong and I'm not going to die in this Year of Sharing. I've always been best at everything in the village school. Now I'm going to be best among the animals. Here's the doctor.

'Hello, Richard. Alone?'

'What do you want, doctor?'

'I want to look at your nose and make sure the recorder's OK. Look up. Look down. Good. After one year we will write down every word from your recorder and make a wonderful book for you. Richard's Year of Sharing.'

'Doctor, I don't want a stupid animal like a cow or a sheep. I want something big, strong and fast, an animal which is not afraid. A clever animal like me.'

'You'll get the animal which is best for you. Does your nose hurt when I touch it here?'

'No.'

'*What can you smell when I open these bottles?*'

'I can smell . . . leaves. Milk. Blood.'

'*OK, your nose is fine. Richard . . . life is easy when you live with people, you know. You will find it harder with animals. I don't know if you're ready. Remember, it's life or death.*'

The doctor's gone. The sky is beginning to get dark. When it's full night, they'll take us – the four of us – to four different animal families. Good. I don't belong in this village. I don't think I belong with *people*. Not people in today's world.

In the old days people were everywhere in the world. Millions of them. They were free to go where they wanted and to do what they wanted. Now there are walls round our villages and we can't go out, and only *animals* are free.

Oh no!

'*Let me just shake hands and say goodbye, Richard.*'

'Dad, you said you wouldn't come.'

'*I'm sorry your mother couldn't come. She had to meet some very important people from all over the world to talk about animals in danger. It was very important business. She wanted to come and say goodbye to you but . . .*'

'Don't try and explain. She's always the same. OK, shake hands and go.'

*Now there are walls round our villages
and we can't go out.*

Dad's gone. It's dark. There's no moon tonight. The stars are very bright.

Soon a doctor will give us something to put us into a deep sleep. When we wake up, we will be with an animal family. The doctor will give me a special smell; I'll smell like a baby in that animal family.

Isn't that terrible? Perhaps the animal family don't *want* another baby . . . but they will smell me and they'll love me. Is love just a special smell, for animals? It's all wrong. I don't like doctors.

Everybody is crying now. Can you hear them? There's no laughing or dancing any more. Here's the doctor coming. In a few minutes I'll be asleep. Goodbye, village. When I see you again, I won't be a child any more.

I can't wait!

2. Deer

Where am I? Where is everybody? Where's the village?

Oh!

I remember.

I've just woken up. I think it's early morning. It's still a little dark because there are trees all around me.

I don't want to sit up and look yet. When I sit up, I will see my animal family. I think I can smell them. I feel a little ill. People don't smell like that.

The trouble is, I've never been near an animal before. We don't have animals in the village, of course. We have to leave animals alone, so we always stay behind our village wall. In the old days people kept cats or dogs in the house; today you would go to prison for keeping an animal.

I'm going to sit up and look at my animal family now. They're deer. I didn't want deer. I wanted a strong animal

They're deer. I didn't want deer.

which can fight, not an animal which runs away like deer. Well, *I'm* not going to run away.

One of the deer is looking at me because I'm moving. I'm trying to stand up but it's difficult. My body is cold; I've never been so cold in my life. I was lying on the wet ground and of course they didn't give me any clothes to wear. I have to move very slowly until I get warm.

There are three deer – no, four. I didn't see the fourth at first because it's very small. I think it's a baby. It's lying beside the deer which is looking at me – I think that's its mother.

The mother is watching me carefully – she thinks I'm her baby too. Poor mother! I'm a strange baby for her to have. There's another deer which looks young – perhaps one year old. The last deer is the biggest – I think he's the father of the two young deer.

There's more light now. The deer are moving around, taking leaves from the trees and eating them. I'm hungry too. I want my breakfast.

What's for breakfast, mother? Don't answer that. I don't think I can eat your food. I know how to find fruit which is good for me and to look in the ground for roots to eat; I learnt all that in the village school. Everybody learns because everybody does the Year of Sharing.

I'll just take a walk and find some food.

Hey, get off! Stop that! What are you doing?

That was the big deer which is the father, I think. He didn't let me take a walk. He ran and pushed me back next to mother. This is terrible. Because of my smell, he thinks I'm a baby. Listen, father – I want to find something to eat!

Deer don't talk much, do they?

✳   ✳   ✳

Sorry I haven't said anything for a long time. There's nothing to say. I'm very, very hungry. I've missed breakfast and I've missed lunch and soon I'm going to miss dinner. It's late afternoon. This deer family likes to move around a lot.

Mother and Baby and I stay together – Father makes sure of that. Brother – the other young deer – sometimes stays with us, but is often alone. Father doesn't like it if Brother follows him.

I've looked for roots in the ground but I haven't found anything. I saw a tree with good fruit on it. I tried to climb the tree but Father knocked me off with his antlers. He was angry. Deer don't climb trees!

So I am HUNGRY.

I'm not cold now. That's because we move around a lot. My arms and legs have a lot of little cuts on them. Well, I'm not wearing clothes and so I keep cutting myself on trees and other things. And my feet hurt.

I didn't think that life with animals would be like this. I thought my new life would be fast, dangerous and exciting.

It isn't. We just walk through the trees. The deer eat while I watch and feel hungry. Then we walk on a little more.

The deer don't talk, they don't make any sounds. Well, sometimes Mother makes a little noise to Baby (and to me because I'm a 'baby' too). And Baby answers with another little noise. But it's nothing special. Mother is saying, 'Where are you?' and Baby is answering, 'I'm here.' That's all.

When Mother asked *me*, 'Where are you?', I didn't answer at first. But she went on asking and asking and asking, and I felt sorry for her. I'm her baby, or she thinks

Because I have nothing to do, I play with Baby.

I am. So then I answered, 'I'm here,' like Baby – I tried to make the same sound as Baby. I'm sure it's right because Mother asks only once now.

Father never talks to Mother. Brother sometimes makes the noise for, 'I'm here,' but nobody listens.

I like Baby. She's sweet. Yes, she's a girl deer. She's soft to touch, she's funny and she's always jumping up and down. She smells of milk.

Because I have nothing to do, I play with Baby. I try to catch her. We run round and round Mother. Then she goes under Mother and I follow, which is funny because

I'm nearly as big as Mother. Mother stops moving because she doesn't want to put her foot down on one of us. When I catch Baby, she suddenly jumps out of my arms. She's like a ball – she uses her four legs to push hard and she jumps high up.

One day of this life is interesting. Not comfortable, but interesting. Two days will be a little boring, I think. After three days I'll want to scream. And I've got a *year* of this life . . .

*   *   *

It's evening now. It suddenly got dark. And cold. I haven't eaten a single thing all day. We swam across a river in the afternoon, so I drank a lot of water then.

These deer are really good at swimming. Baby can swim too – but Mother and Father helped Baby and me.

The deer family is going to spend the night here. All right. I would like to go and look for something to put over myself, to keep myself warm. I don't think Father will let me. Let's see.

I was right. Father didn't let me. I'll just have to be cold.

It's spring – the Year of Sharing usually begins in spring. I don't know what a *winter* night will be like. Perhaps I will learn to keep warm by then.

Brother is asleep. Baby is lying beside Mother. Father is walking in a slow circle around us. He's listening and smelling the wind. He'll make sure we're not in danger.

I'm sitting on the ground, with my arms round my body, trying to keep warm, but I'm shaking with cold.

Baby is drinking Mother's milk.

For the first time today I feel lonely. I don't often feel lonely. I don't need people. I think it's the dark and the cold and being hungry and feeling sorry for myself and listening to Baby drinking Mother's warm milk and knowing that I can't do that.

Mother just said, 'Where are you?' to me.

I made the sound which means, 'I'm here.'

*   *   *

I'm falling asleep while I speak. I drank Mother's milk. I'm lying with Baby next to Mother and it's very warm. I don't feel lonely. Good night.

I'm lying with Baby next to Mother.

3. Wolves

I've just lived through the worst two weeks of my life. I feel a lot better now; that's why I'm speaking again. I didn't want to say anything when there wasn't anything good to say.

It rained most of the time. When it wasn't raining, the water was still falling off the leaves of the trees. I was wet, cold, tired and hungry all the time. I was ill. My head hurt, my stomach hurt, my feet and legs hurt and I was always getting little cuts on my body. Worst of all I missed home; I wanted to be back in the village.

That's still true. I don't want to be here. Deer are not people. I said I didn't need people, but I think I was wrong. It's hard to *think* when you can't talk to anybody.

I'm friends with Baby and Brother. I like both of them. Baby is sweet and Brother is afraid of nothing. The two older deer are afraid of *everything* – afraid of birds singing, birds not singing, a cloud going over the sun, a leaf falling. When they're afraid, they jump. They're *always* jumping!

When Mother thinks we're in danger, she pushes me and Baby with her nose. She takes us to dark places in the forest where the trees are crowded together. We move quickly and quietly, in and out of the trees. I'm beginning to feel afraid of everything now. It's stupid. I've not seen

I was wet, cold, tired and hungry all the time.

anything to be afraid of.

I'm getting thin because I don't eat very much. I find a few wild vegetables and a little fruit every day and I drink Mother's milk before I sleep. That's all.

These deer eat all the time. They like eating from some

trees, not others. Mother has to help Baby to get leaves and fruit. She tries to help me too, but deer food is not my food. I can't eat it.

Mother is unhappy because I'm not eating well. Poor Mother! I'm angry with her all day, but I sleep with her like a baby at night. It's strange. My feelings for Mother are very strong – stronger than my feelings for my real mother – both good and bad feelings.

Father doesn't come near us very often. He keeps walking around, up and down. He stands tall and looks through the trees. He puts his nose high up and smells carefully. He gets the best things to eat and he pushes the rest of the family away if they try to eat near him.

I didn't wear clothes for the first week and that was terrible because we're in the forest all the time, and I couldn't stop getting cuts. So I made some clothes out of leaves. They're not very good clothes and I have to keep making new ones, but they stop most of the cuts and also keep me warm – well, not *very* warm, but I'm not as cold as before.

So I'm feeling better. A little warmer, a little more food in my stomach and my body doesn't hurt now.

And I'm stronger and quicker and I can hear and see better too. If you can't talk to anybody, you *look* and *listen* and *smell*.

Brother and I are always trying to see who can jump

higher. I lose – most of the time. But I'm getting better.
We both enjoy it.

There's no rain this morning, which is really wonderful.
Up above there's only blue sky between the trees. Down
here it's not warm, but it's not cold and wet any more.

Ow!

Something happened! Father ran up and knocked me
over with his antlers. He wants me to be quiet. Now I'm
speaking *very* softly. All the deer have stopped eating. Only
Father is moving now, walking very slowly, putting one
foot down carefully before moving the next foot.

It's very, very quiet. Not a sound anywhere. Why is it
so quiet? Why are there no birds singing?

Oh! Now I can see it. It's an animal coming through
the trees, not quickly, not slowly. It's a wolf!

It's a wolf!

There's only one wolf. Oops! Mother just pushed me because she wants me to move. Now she's pushing Baby. The family is moving away, going deeper into the forest. Brother doesn't want to run away, and he's looking at me. Will I run away?

No, I'm not going to run. It's stupid. There are four deer and me against just one wolf. We can fight and the *wolf* will run away.

I'm staying. I've got a big stick and some stones and I can fight this wolf alone if I have to.

Father has gone. Mother's coming back for me – no, she isn't. She's stopped, she can't leave Baby.

Brother's coming to stand with me. Mother and Baby have gone. There's only Brother, me and the wolf now. I'm not afraid. Let's see how the wolf likes getting a stone on its nose. Take that!

I missed him! I'm good at throwing stones, but the wolf jumped to one side very fast. Now I'm throwing each stone as hard as I can. The wolf's jumping all over the place, but he's not running away. Well, I've still got my stick. Brother can use his feet to fight with. We'll be all right.

Oh no!

Two more wolves are coming, and they're coming *fast*. Brother, go! Get out of here! That's right.

Now I'm alone. There's only one thing to do.

There's only Brother, me and the wolf now.

I nearly died. I made a very big mistake when I decided to stand and fight. That's what a person does, not a deer. I'm a deer. I smell like a deer and so wolves think I'm a deer too.

I feel bad. I feel *small*, and unimportant. I'm not a person. I'm just an animal. If another animal is stronger than me, it can kill me. I didn't understand that before.

I saved Brother; I'm happy about that. The first wolf ran at me, very fast; I suddenly jumped right over him. I'm wonderful at jumping. After two weeks with deer, anybody would be wonderful.

The wolf didn't turn very quickly. I looked around for the other two wolves and saw that they weren't coming for me, they were following Brother. This was bad.

I screamed, because I wanted the wolves to think I was afraid; then they would follow me, not Brother. But when I screamed, I knew I really was afraid, and the wolves knew it too. That was terrible. All three wolves stopped and ran straight at me.

Yes, I was afraid! I dropped the stick and ran like a . . . like a deer. There was a big tree in front of me and in seconds I was at the top of it.

And here I am. The wolves sat under my tree for hours with a hungry look in their eyes. They left not long ago, just before it got dark.

And this is where I'm staying. I can't find the deer in the dark. I can't lie down with Mother and drink her milk. I don't think I can sleep in a tree . . . but I'll try. And I'm sorry Brother nearly died because of me.

Will I see my deer family again?

All three wolves ran straight at me.

4. Killing a wolf

It's morning and I'm still up in the tree. I didn't sleep all night. I'm hungry, tired, cold and angry. I'm going to climb down the tree and look for some food.

* * *

That's better. I can't think when I'm hungry.

When I remember how I ran away from those wolves, I feel angry and my face gets hot. Why did I run away? I wasn't afraid!

I screamed and ran away to save Brother, of course. That's why. I don't want to go back to the deer family. If I'm not living with deer, I don't have to run away from anything. I can live alone for my Year of Sharing. I can find food, water, places to sleep and leaves to make clothes with. I don't need the deer; life is more difficult with them.

I have decided not to follow the deer and I feel happier now. I won't get lonely or bored; I'm better alone.

If a wolf comes, I'll kill it. I can fight wolves if I have sticks and stones. When I find the dead body of an animal, I will cut it up and use it to make something for killing wolves – a catapult which will shoot stones.

I feel *much* better.

* * *

Things have changed again. I'm back with the deer.

I was sitting on the ground, cutting a stick with a stone, when I heard Mother calling. She was far away. I only heard her because it was very quiet all around.

She was calling, 'Where are you? Where are you?' and I knew she was calling *me*.

It was terrible. I began crying. She's only a deer. I smell like a baby deer to her, but I'm not really.

I answered, 'I'm here!'

Mother heard me and ran to me. She was calling all the time. She came through the trees with Baby behind her and I stood up, still crying, and I . . .

I don't want to talk about it any more. Sometimes I don't understand myself. I never put my arms round my real mother like that, and Mother is only a *deer*.

What could I do? I walked with Mother and Baby through the forest for a long time until we found Father and Brother. Father stopped eating and hit Mother with his antlers. He was angry; he wanted her to be near him all the time.

When Father came up to me, I thought he would hit me too, but he didn't. He smelt me carefully, then touched me softly with his head. To him, I'm just a baby.

Brother jumped straight up and down; he was so happy to see me again. I was surprised how happy I was to see *him* too.

In the last few days we have walked and walked. When

the others want to stop and eat, Father keeps us moving. We have swum across rivers, pushed through trees, run across open ground and moved back into trees again. I know why – we all know.

There's a wolf, or wolves, following us. It calls – a long, hungry howling, often at night. It's following our smell. That's why Father tries to go through water as often as possible – smells are lost in water.

I'm busy with my special answer to this danger – I'm making weapons. I break up stones into little pieces. Some pieces of stone are really sharp and will cut like a knife. I've put them on long sticks to make spears.

I found a dead animal and cut off its skin, then I cut the skin into long, thin pieces. Now I have a good catapult; I can kill wolves.

Brother's teaching Baby to jump as high as she can. That's his job. Mother teaches Baby about eating and smelling things and cleaning herself. Father doesn't have time to teach Baby. He's always walking round. He's smelling, listening, watching the trees, waiting for something bad to happen. He always knows the best place to go next, because he never stops thinking about it.

Brother, Baby and I often jump together, moving in sudden, high jumps across the ground. I'm beginning to understand why deer jump so much. A jump catches the eye of a wolf. When a wolf runs after a deer, another deer

I've put the stones on long sticks to make spears.

will jump and the wolf will turn to look at it. Then a third deer will jump. The wolf turns again. Each jump takes the deer away from the wolf and the wolf can't decide which deer to follow. It's clever.

Yesterday something bad happened. Baby did a good, high jump but when she came down, she gave a little scream.

She tried to walk and screamed again, a little, high scream. Mother ran to her and Father stood not far away and watched.

I couldn't see what was wrong at first; Mother didn't want anyone to come near. In the end I lay down next to Baby and saw what it was – a stick from a tree was deep inside Baby's leg and Mother's teeth couldn't pull it out. Mother didn't let me touch it.

Baby could only walk on three legs and she got tired very quickly. Father tried to move on again, away from the wolf, but Mother wanted to stay with Baby. Father pushed Mother and she followed him . . . but then went

A stick from a tree was deep inside Baby's leg.

back to Baby. Father went back and pushed Mother again.

In the end Father took Baby to a dark place where she could hide under leaves. It was near a river and the ground was wet. That would hide Baby's smell from the wolf.

Then Father pushed us all away. But when we left, we could hear Baby calling after us. She didn't understand. Her calls said, 'I'm here! I'm here!'

Father didn't let Mother go back. We walked on. The howl of a wolf came through the trees from far away. I thought of a wolf finding Baby.

I just couldn't leave her.

I stopped. Mother called me but Father was pushing her to go on. I stayed still and they went into the trees and I couldn't see them any more. There are no goodbyes with deer.

I ran back to Baby and she stopped calling. She was happy.

I put my weapons on the ground – my catapult and spears. When I touched Baby's leg, she didn't like it; it hurt a lot. She didn't let me touch it again.

So I lay down heavily on top of her. I held the stick in her leg and moved it slowly and carefully. I pulled and turned it until it came out, all of it. Then I went and carried water in my hand from the river to wash the place on her leg. That was all I could do.

I brought leaves for Baby to eat, and water for her to

drink. When it got dark, I lay down with her and we slept, keeping warm together.

I've just looked at her leg and I think it's getting better. But she can't walk on it yet. We have to stay here for a few days. Then we will follow the deer family. I think I can find them. I can smell where they have been, I can see where they have walked and I understand how Father thinks.

With luck I can find them.

I turned, holding the catapult, and looked at the wolves.

The wolves found us two days later. It was evening, just before dark. Two wolves walked out of the trees and saw me carrying food to Baby. They were thin and hungry wolves. I don't think they have eaten for a long time.

My weapons were under the leaves with Baby. I dropped the food and ran and quickly got a catapult and a few stones. Of course, the wolves thought I was running away and they came to get me.

I turned, holding the catapult, and looked at them, and they stopped in surprise. Why wasn't I running away?

I felt cold inside, but not afraid. 'Which one of you shall I kill?' I asked them. 'Which one of you will die first?'

The wolves heard my cold voice. They knew I was dangerous, but they were hungry. They came slowly and they didn't make a sound. I shot a stone from the catapult and it hit one wolf on the eye. The wolf screamed. I followed that with more stones until a very big one cut its head open. The wolf fell over on its side and didn't move.

The other wolf jumped, turned and ran back into the trees. I looked at the dead wolf on the ground and felt sorry.

From the trees came a long, lonely howl.

I waited until it was dark and then Baby and I began walking. Baby walked for a while and then rested. I couldn't follow the deer family in the dark because I couldn't see anything and the smells were cold. But I thought I knew where Father would go.

There was a moon. I decided we had to walk all night because the other wolf was still out there somewhere.

Baby's leg was doing well; I was happy about that. An hour later, we were far from the dark hiding place under the leaves. The wolf wouldn't find us now.

There was a howl in the night. Then another howl, and another. Three, four, five, six howls – from different sides. The wolves were far away, but there were lots of them. Too many.

And so I learnt something new. Wolves have families too – big families. If you kill one wolf, the family wants to find the killer. We were in trouble.

5.   The wolves are coming

I don't like danger, but if you live through it, you feel good.

Just now we're resting on the other side of a large lake. The wolves sound very far away and I think we're OK. I've done everything possible to make sure they can't follow us.

When I heard all those wolves howling in the dark, I touched Baby and said, 'Stand very quietly and listen.'

Of course Baby didn't understand, but she stopped and didn't move. I was listening for water – a river or anything. I couldn't hear water, just the wind in the trees and a wolf singing to the moon.

So I tried *smelling* for water. My nose is wonderful at smelling now and, yes, I could smell something wet. When I turned round, I knew where the wet smell was coming from.

'We'll be fine, Baby,' I said. I put my hand on her head. 'But we can't stop any more until we get to the water.

Can you run with that leg?'

Baby's leg was hurting, but she ran when I ran. She was afraid of losing me. I was all she had.

The wolves howled, not all the time but sometimes. I didn't know how near they were. Each howl went on for nearly a minute. Sometimes I didn't know if they were behind or in front of us.

I saw light through the trees. I hurried and Baby came after me. Soon we came to open ground, and there it was – moonlight on water! Not a river, but a big lake.

'It's a long swim, Baby,' I told her, 'but if we stay here, we'll die.'

Baby wasn't afraid of water. She followed me in and swam easily beside me. It was easier for her to swim than run with her bad leg.

How far was it to the other side? I don't know, but it took us a long, long time. It was more difficult for me than Baby in the end. I'm a walking, climbing animal; deer are running, jumping, swimming animals. My arms and legs hurt, my body felt heavy and I swam more and more slowly. But Baby was always there beside me, touching me all the time, her legs moving quickly in the water. She was warm, while I was cold, and that helped me.

The moon went behind clouds and we swam in the dark. I was happy about that because I was afraid the wolves would see us. When my feet hit stones underneath me,

I knew the water wasn't deep any more. I stood up. A minute later Baby was walking too. We walked out of the water. My legs couldn't hold me up. I half fell and lay on

My legs couldn't hold me up.

the ground and felt very happy. Baby lay beside me, wet but warm. I slept for a little while.

I've just woken up. We have to begin moving soon. It's still night, but we must be far away from here by morning. Some of the ground is soft. Soft ground is dangerous because the wolves can see where we have gone. We must go on the hard, stony places.

It's wonderful! We're back with Mother, Father and Brother. I wasn't really sure that I could find them.

When the deer family left us three days ago, I saw some hills to the north. Father always hides in the trees when there's danger, and up there on the hills there are a lot of big, dark trees. Just right for Father.

I had good luck. When we got to the hills, we didn't have to look very far. I could hear the deer eating before I smelt them.

Baby went in a funny, jumping run up to Mother. She kept one foot off the ground; it was still hurting. Mother and Baby touched heads and made noises. Father came and smelt me while Brother watched. Father doesn't usually get too near anyone in the family, but he stood nearly touching me. I think he was saying thank you, and my eyes were wet.

I spoke to Father. 'We must go deeper into the trees. There are wolves behind us trying to follow us.'

Father came and smelt me while Brother watched.

Father didn't like me talking. He moved away and began eating again. Then Brother came. He wanted to play.

'I'm too tired,' I explained. 'I want to get deeper into the trees, then I want to sleep.'

Nobody did what I wanted. They didn't understand about the wolves, and the leaves were sweet. Baby drank Mother's milk and Brother and Father went on eating.

So I slept where I was.

It's afternoon now. We're still here. It's warm and bright and there's a blue sky. I'm not afraid any more. I was just tired. The wolves have lost us and we're OK.

*　　*　　*

I was wrong. The wolves followed us. I could hear many wolves howling. They were far away, but coming.

I was angry with myself. How did the wolves find us? Baby and I tried so hard – we ran, we swam across water, and we stayed away from soft ground, but it didn't help.

Then I saw something which explained it. There were flies walking around a drop of blood on the ground. The cut on Baby's leg was open again, and the wolves were following the strong smell of blood.

It was too late to go deep into the trees now. The wolves would find us. I looked at the four deer – my family – and I knew I couldn't let them die. There was an answer. It was dangerous, but I had to do it.

First I cleaned Baby's cut again and put leaves on it to stop the blood. Then I cut myself – a small cut on the leg, with a sharp stone.

'You go up there,' I said to Father, 'up into the trees and I'll go along open ground, over there. The wolves will follow my blood. If the wolves don't catch me, I'll wait for a few days and then I'll find you again. Do you understand?'

Of course he didn't, but he understood the danger that was coming. Brother wanted to come with me. This time

Father got angry with him and pushed him up the hill.
No goodbyes, of course.

I began running down the hill where there were no trees.
I looked back and I couldn't see the deer.

I was stronger after my sleep and I ran fast. I knew where
I was going. There was a high, rocky hill about two miles
away – I could climb it, but wolves couldn't. But could I
get there before the wolves found me?

No goodbyes, of course.

I ran and didn't look back. After ten minutes I wanted to stop and rest, but then I heard the howls. I looked back and the wolves were running behind me.

So I didn't rest. I ran and they ran. I was afraid, really afraid. I couldn't feel my legs. 'Don't fall, keep going,' I said to myself.

I ran to save my life. When I came to the rocks, I didn't stop; I climbed up faster than a wild cat. One wolf hit another wolf just below me and fell over. Their angry howls rang in my ears. I went up and up until I came to a place where I could rest. I sat with my back to the rock and looked down. Wolves everywhere . . .

I sat with my back to the rock and looked down.
Wolves everywhere . . .

38

I'm here and they can't get me now. When I've rested, I'll climb up to the top and I'll be OK.

No, wait – perhaps I'll stay here until morning. I need to sleep. I'll feel better after a good sleep. I don't feel very well. I can't remember the last time I ate something. *Listen* to those wolves! They're hungry too, of course. I'm an animal just like them.

RICHARD'S FATHER SPEAKS:

What happened? We don't know.

When Richard's Year of Sharing finished, I went to bring him home. I followed the radio call of his recorder. I found the recorder at the bottom of the hill where he tried to escape from the wolves. The recorder was there, but not Richard.

Did he fall while he was sleeping? Did the accident happen next morning while he was climbing to the top? I don't know.

I am very unhappy. The village says we can now have another child. But I don't want one. I cannot say more.

RICHARD'S MOTHER SPEAKS:

Richard was a difficult boy. He was angry and he wanted to bring back the old world, the world where people took everything and animals had nothing. But in the end he learnt to share. He learnt that people are animals too, and that the world belongs not just to people, but to all animals. It is a hard lesson to learn, but we must all learn it. Now my son is dead. But the people of this village, and their children, and their children's children, will never forget him.

GLOSSARY

antlers two long hard things which grow on a deer's head

catapult a stick like the letter 'Y', with a piece of elastic, which you can use for throwing stones

climb to move up something high like a tree or a mountain

deer a large wild animal with long thin legs, which eats leaves and can run fast

feelings what you think and feel about somebody or something

forest a large number of trees growing close together

howl *(n)* the long loud cry of a wolf

keep (doing) to do something again and again; not stop doing it

lake a big piece of water with land all around it

let to allow someone to do something

make sure to do something because you want to be sure that something happens

miss *(v)* to feel unhappy when something or someone is not there

record *(v)* to put sounds on a machine which can play them back later

recorder a machine which records words or music

rock stone; very hard part of the ground

root the part of a plant which grows under the ground

save to keep somebody from danger, or to stop somebody dying

share *(v)* to use or have something with other people, not to keep it for yourself

sharing having something together with other people

sharp if something is sharp, it will cut things

41

skin   the outside covering of the body of a person or animal

spear   a weapon made from a long stick with a sharp point at the end

straight   by the shortest way; not turning left or right and not stopping

throw (past tense **threw**)   to use your hand to send something quickly through the air

weapon   something which can hurt or kill people (e.g. a gun)

wolf   a wild animal which looks like a large dog

The Year of Sharing

ACTIVITIES

Before Reading

1 Read the story introduction on the first page of the book and the back cover. How much do you know now about the story? Tick one box for each sentence.

	YES	NO
1 Richard lives in the 1990s.	☐	☐
2 Richard lives in a big city.	☐	☐
3 Richard wants a fast car.	☐	☐
4 Richard is twelve years old.	☐	☐
5 Richard is going to live with animals.	☐	☐
6 Only a few children go and live with animals.	☐	☐

2 What will Richard's life be like in the forest? Can you guess? Make sentences, using some of these words.

food, clothes, sleep, friends, mother and father, bicycle

3 What is going to happen in the story? Can you guess? Tick one box for each sentence.

	YES	NO
1 Richard will live with a family of cats.	☐	☐
2 Richard will come home after a few weeks.	☐	☐
3 Richard will kill an animal.	☐	☐
4 Richard will die.	☐	☐

While Reading

Read Chapter 1. Are these sentences true (T) or false (F)? Rewrite the false ones with the correct information.

1 Richard and three more children are going to do their Year of Sharing.
2 Richard has got a recorder in his ear.
3 Richard's friends are at the party with him.
4 Richard wants to live with a family of sheep.
5 Richard's mother came to say goodbye to him.
6 Richard is going to go to sleep and wake up with an animal family.

Read Chapter 2, and then answer these questions.

1 Which animal family did Richard wake up with?
2 Why was Richard cold?
3 What food did Richard see?
4 Why didn't he eat it?
5 What do the deer noises mean?
6 Who did Richard play with?
7 What did the family do in the afternoon?
8 Where did Richard fall asleep?
9 What did he do before he fell asleep?

Read Chapter 3. Here are some untrue sentences about it. Change them into true sentences.

1 Richard didn't want to be back in the village.
2 Richard didn't like Baby and Brother.
3 Richard ate a lot of fruit and vegetables every day.
4 Mother knocked Richard over with her antlers.
5 Richard saw a cat coming through the trees.
6 Richard threw stones at Baby.
7 Two wolves were following Richard.
8 The three wolves ran away from Richard.
9 Brother climbed a tree.

Read Chapter 4, and then answer these questions.

Why

1 . . . did Richard scream and run away?
2 . . . did Richard go back to the deer family?
3 . . . did Father hit Mother with his antlers?
4 . . . did Brother jump up and down?
5 . . . did Father go through water as often as possible?
6 . . . did Richard break up stones into little pieces?
7 . . . did Richard make a catapult?
8 . . . did Baby scream?
9 . . . did Father leave Baby near a river?
10 . . . did Richard run back to Baby?
11 . . . were the wolves surprised?

Before you read Chapter 5, can you guess what happens? The title of the chapter is *The wolves are coming*. Tick one box for each sentence.

	YES	NO
1 Richard and Baby find the deer family again.	☐	☐
2 The wolves kill Baby.	☐	☐
3 The wolves kill Richard.	☐	☐
4 Richard kills a lot of wolves.	☐	☐
5 The deer run away from the wolves.	☐	☐

Read Chapter 5, then put these sentences in the right order.

1 He knew they were following the smell of blood.

2 Then he ran very fast to a hill two miles away.

3 It was a big lake and he and Baby swam across it.

4 So he cut himself on the leg because he wanted the wolves to follow him, not his deer family.

5 The next day, he and Baby found their deer family on the hills.

6 So he used his nose to find water.

7 He climbed up the rocks just in time.

8 Richard wanted to make sure that the wolves couldn't follow him.

9 But the wolves were waiting for him at the bottom.

10 When they got to the other side, Richard fell asleep.

11 Later, Richard heard the wolves howling again.

After Reading

1 Here is a possible ending to the story. Match these parts of sentences and put them in the correct order to make a paragraph of five sentences. Use these linking words.

and / and / because / because / so / when

1 . . . he was frightened.
2 he suddenly fell all the way to the bottom of the rocks
3 . . . he was near the top,
4 Richard fell asleep
5 . . . tried to climb to the top of the rocks.
6 He also felt ill and hungry
7 . . . the wolves jumped on him.
8 . . . he didn't have any breakfast.
9 The next morning, he woke up early
10 . . . he was very tired.
11 The wolves were still watching him,

2 Which is your favourite animal? Choose from this list, or use a dictionary. Would you like to live with your favourite animal? Explain why, or why not.

bird, cat, cow, deer, fish, horse, sheep, wolf

3 Here is a new illustration for the story. Find the best place
in the story to put the picture, and answer these questions.

The picture goes on page _____.

1 Why was Richard in the tree?
2 What did the wolves do?
3 What did Richard do after that?

Now write a caption for the illustration.

Caption: _____

49

4 **How did Richard live in the forest? Make sentences like this from the chart.**

Example: *He ate roots from the ground.*

	clothes		Mother
eat	fruit		animal skin
make	spears	from	trees
drink	milk		leaves
	a catapult		sticks and stones

5 **Match the sentences with the deer. Then use the sentences to write a short description of each deer. Join them with *and* where possible and use pronouns (*he, she, his, her*).**

Baby, Brother, Father, Mother

1 _____ makes a noise that means 'Where are you?'

2 _____ is soft to touch.

3 _____ is afraid of nothing.

4 _____ gets the best things to eat.

5 _____ is funny.

6 _____ never talks to Mother.

7 _____ helps Baby to get leaves and fruit.

8 _____ is always jumping up and down.

9 _____ smells of milk.

10 _____ teaches Baby to jump as high as she can.

11 _____ is always walking around.

12 _____ teaches Baby about eating and smelling.

6 **Do you agree (A) or disagree (D) with these sentences? Explain why.**

   1 Richard's mother and father didn't love him.
   2 Richard was right to be angry and bored with his life in the village.
   3 The deer family was a better family for Richard than his real family.
   4 Richard was wrong to try and save the deer family.
   5 In today's world, people have everything and animals have nothing.

7 **Choose one of these sentences and complete it with your own ideas.**

   1 The Year of Sharing is a stupid and dangerous idea because _____.
   2 The Year of Sharing is a good idea because _____.

8 **Richard's world is different from our world today. Write five sentences about the differences. Use some of these words.**

   cars, bicycles, meat, villages, cities, people, animals, factories, cats and dogs, houses, children

9 **How do you imagine the world of the future? Will it be like Richard's world? Write five sentences about 'your' future.**

ABOUT THE AUTHOR

Harry Gilbert was born in Canada in 1946 and came to England when he was a baby. After university, he travelled in many parts of the world, doing various jobs, including teaching English as a Foreign Language. He is married, with one daughter, and now lives and teaches in London. As well as *The Year of Sharing*, he has written *The Star Zoo* (at Stage 3) for the Oxford Bookworms Library, and he has also written several books for English children.

Harry Gilbert fell in love with science fiction when he was eleven years old, and spent the next five years reading every science-fiction story he could find, and also writing his own stories. He says that getting ideas for stories is hard work. The ideas for *The Year of Sharing* and *The Star Zoo* came to him while he was watching students during their examinations.

OXFORD BOOKWORMS LIBRARY

Classics • Crime & Mystery • Factfiles • Fantasy & Horror
Human Interest • Playscripts • Thriller & Adventure
True Stories • World Stories

The OXFORD BOOKWORMS LIBRARY provides enjoyable reading in English, with a wide range of classic and modern fiction, non-fiction, and plays. It includes original and adapted texts in seven carefully graded language stages, which take learners from beginner to advanced level. An overview is given on the next pages.

All Stage 1 titles are available as audio recordings, as well as over eighty other titles from Starter to Stage 6. All Starters and many titles at Stages 1 to 4 are specially recommended for younger learners. Every Bookworm is illustrated, and Starters and Factfiles have full-colour illustrations.

The OXFORD BOOKWORMS LIBRARY also offers extensive support. Each book contains an introduction to the story, notes about the author, a glossary, and activities. Additional resources include tests and worksheets, and answers for these and for the activities in the books. There is advice on running a class library, using audio recordings, and the many ways of using Oxford Bookworms in reading programmes. Resource materials are available on the website <www.oup.com/bookworms>.

The *Oxford Bookworms Collection* is a series for advanced learners. It consists of volumes of short stories by well-known authors, both classic and modern. Texts are not abridged or adapted in any way, but carefully selected to be accessible to the advanced student.

You can find details and a full list of titles in the *Oxford Bookworms Library Catalogue* and *Oxford English Language Teaching Catalogues*, and on the website <www.oup.com/bookworms>.

THE OXFORD BOOKWORMS LIBRARY
GRADING AND SAMPLE EXTRACTS

STARTER • 250 HEADWORDS

present simple – present continuous – imperative –
can/cannot, must – going to (future) – simple gerunds ...

Her phone is ringing – but where is it?

Sally gets out of bed and looks in her bag. No phone. She looks under the bed. No phone. Then she looks behind the door. There is her phone. Sally picks up her phone and answers it. *Sally's Phone*

STAGE 1 • 400 HEADWORDS

... past simple – coordination with and, but, or –
subordination with before, after, when, because, so ...

I knew him in Persia. He was a famous builder and I worked with him there. For a time I was his friend, but not for long. When he came to Paris, I came after him – I wanted to watch him. He was a very clever, very dangerous man. *The Phantom of the Opera*

STAGE 2 • 700 HEADWORDS

... present perfect – will (future) – (don't) have to, must not, could –
comparison of adjectives – simple if clauses – past continuous –
tag questions – ask/tell + infinitive ...

While I was writing these words in my diary, I decided what to do. I must try to escape. I shall try to get down the wall outside. The window is high above the ground, but I have to try. I shall take some of the gold with me – if I escape, perhaps it will be helpful later. *Dracula*

… *should, may* – present perfect continuous – *used to* – past perfect –
causative – relative clauses – indirect statements …

Of course, it was most important that no one should see
Colin, Mary, or Dickon entering the secret garden. So Colin
gave orders to the gardeners that they must all keep away
from that part of the garden in future. ***The Secret Garden***

STAGE 4 • 1400 HEADWORDS

… past perfect continuous – passive (simple forms) –
would conditional clauses – indirect questions –
relatives with *where/when* – gerunds after prepositions/phrases …

I was glad. Now Hyde could not show his face to the world
again. If he did, every honest man in London would be proud
to report him to the police. ***Dr Jekyll and Mr Hyde***

STAGE 5 • 1800 HEADWORDS

… future continuous – future perfect –
passive (modals, continuous forms) –
would have conditional clauses – modals + perfect infinitive …

If he had spoken Estella's name, I would have hit him. I was so
angry with him, and so depressed about my future, that I could
not eat the breakfast. Instead I went straight to the old house.
Great Expectations

STAGE 6 • 2500 HEADWORDS

… passive (infinitives, gerunds) – advanced modal meanings –
clauses of concession, condition

When I stepped up to the piano, I was confident. It was as if I
knew that the prodigy side of me really did exist. And when I
started to play, I was so caught up in how lovely I looked that
I didn't worry how I would sound. ***The Joy Luck Club***

Voodoo Island

MICHAEL DUCKWORTH

Mr James Conway wants to make money. He wants to build new houses and shops – and he wants to build them on an old graveyard, on the island of Haiti.

There is only one old man who still visits the graveyard; and Mr Conway is not afraid of one old man.

But the old man has friends – friends in the graveyard, friends who lie dead, under the ground. And when Mr Conway starts to build his houses, he makes the terrible mistake of disturbing the sleep of the dead …

The Piano

ROSEMARY BORDER

One day, a farmer tells a farm boy to take everything out of an old building and throw it away. 'It's all rubbish,' he says.

In the middle of all the rubbish, the boy finds a beautiful old piano. He has never played before, but now, when his fingers touch the piano, he begins to play. He closes his eyes and the music comes to him – and the music moves his fingers.

When he opens his eyes again, he knows that his life is changed for ever …